Read for a Better World™

DUMP TRUCKS

A First Look

ZELDA WAGNER

Lerner Publications ◆ Minneapolis

Educator Toolbox

Reading books is a great way for kids to express what they're interested in. Before reading this title, ask the reader these questions:

What do you think this book is about? Look at the cover for clues.

What do you already know about dump trucks?

What do you want to learn about dump trucks?

Let's Read Together

Encourage the reader to use the pictures to understand the text.

Point out when the reader successfully sounds out a word.

Praise the reader for recognizing sight words such as *is* and *at*.

TABLE OF CONTENTS

Dump Trucks

Dump trucks are big.

Where might workers use dump trucks?

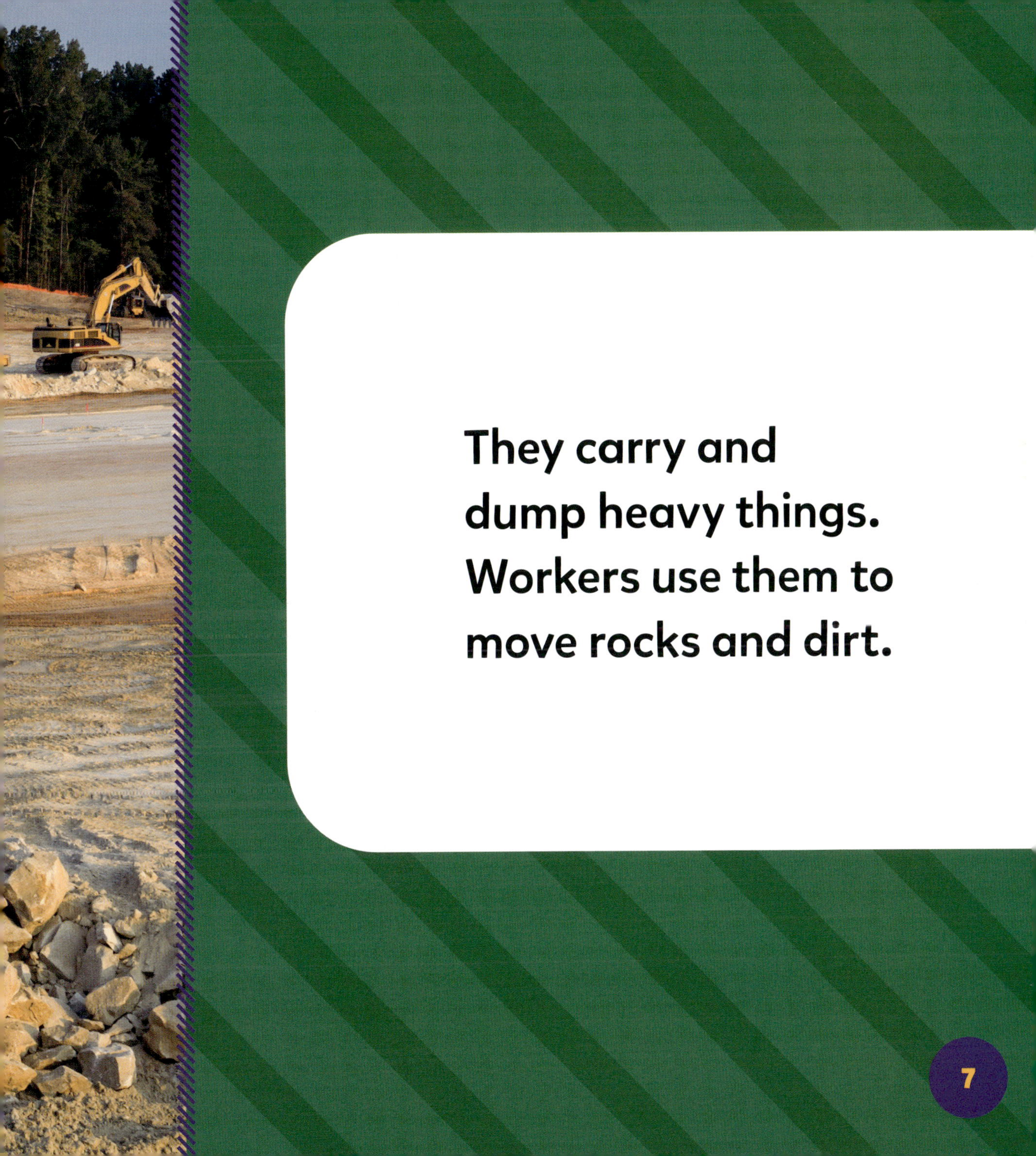

They carry and dump heavy things. Workers use them to move rocks and dirt.

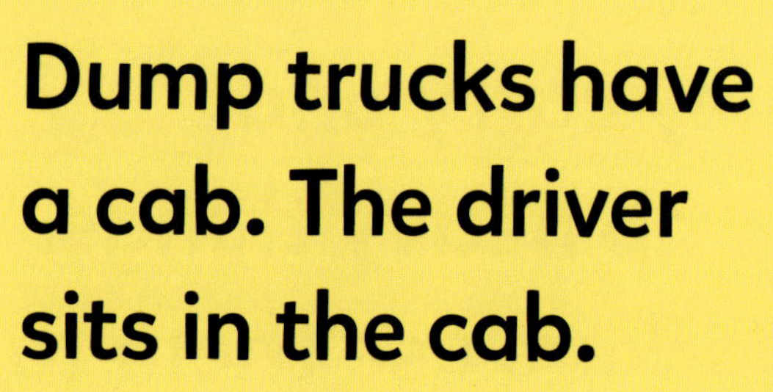

Dump trucks have a cab. The driver sits in the cab.

The bed is at the back.

Dirt fills the bed. The dump truck takes the dirt away.

The bed tips up. The dirt comes out.

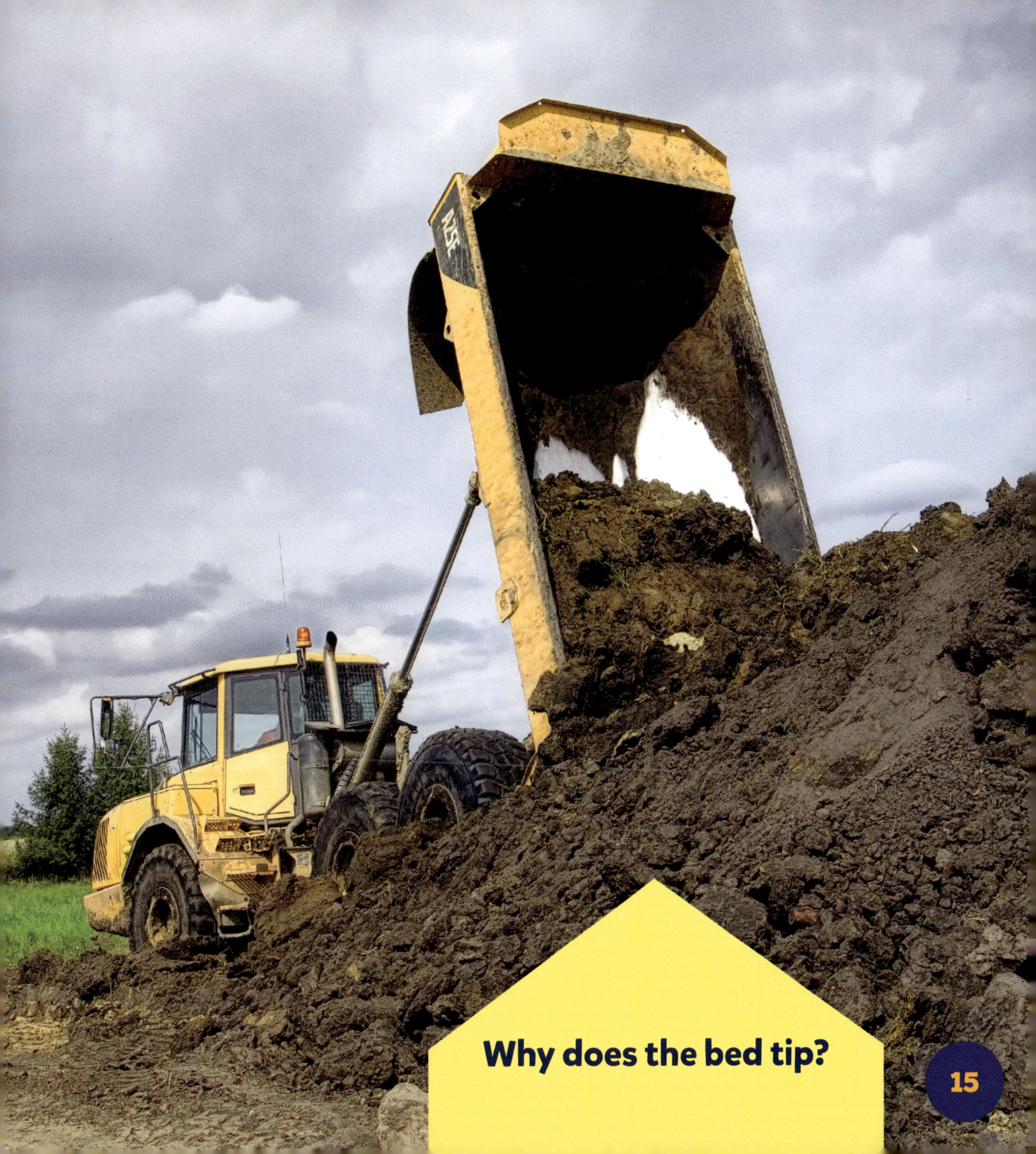

Why does the bed tip?

The biggest dump trucks work at mines.

The driver uses a ladder or steps to get to the cab.

Big dump trucks from mines are wide. They are too big to go on roads.

Why do you think mines need big dump trucks?

Dump trucks help workers do big jobs!

You Connect!

Have you ever seen a dump truck?

Would you want to drive a dump truck?

How can you learn more about dump trucks?

STEM Snapshot

Encourage students to think and ask questions like scientists. Ask the reader:

What is something you learned about dump trucks?

What is something you noticed about dump truck parts?

What is something you still want to learn about dump trucks?

Photo Glossary

Learn More

Amoroso, Cynthia. *Dump Trucks*. Parker, CO: Child's World, 2023.

Earley, Ryan. *Dump Trucks*. Coral Springs, FL: Seahorse, 2023.

Wagner, Zelda. *Backhoes: A First Look*. Minneapolis: Lerner Publications, 2025.

Index

Photo Acknowledgments

Image credits: kozmoat98/Getty Images, pp. 4–5; Cavan Images/Getty Images, pp. 6–7; shotbydave/Getty Images, pp. 8-9; Dimitri Disterheft/Alamy, pp. 10–11; ooyoo/Getty Images, pp. 12–13; Alexandre Patchine/Alamy, p. 12 (bottom); Krzysztof Grzymajlo/Alamy, pp. 14–15; Monty Rakusen/Getty Images, p. 16; buranatrakul/Getty Images, p. 17; Lakeview_Images/Getty Images, pp. 18–19; ewg3D/Getty Images, p. 20. Cover image: kozmoat98/Getty Images.

Lerner Publications Company
An imprint of Lerner Publishing Group, Inc.
241 First Avenue North
Minneapolis, MN 55401 USA

For reading levels and more information, look up this title at www.lernerbooks.com.

Main body text set in Mikado Medium. Typeface provided by Hannes von Doehren.

Library of Congress Cataloging-in-Publication Data

Names: Wagner, Zelda, 2000- author.
Title: Dump trucks : a first look / Zelda Wagner.
Description: Minneapolis : Lerner Publications, [2025] | Series: Read about construction vehicles | Includes bibliographical references and index. | Audience: Ages 5–8 | Summary: "Dump trucks carry and dump heavy loads! They're used at mines, construction sites, and more. Young readers will enjoy learning more about what they do and how they're used"— Provided by publisher.
Identifiers: LCCN 2024009536 (print) | LCCN 2024009537 (ebook) | ISBN 9798765647844 (lib. bdg.) | ISBN 9798765662229 (pbk.) | ISBN 9798765657270 (epub)
Subjects: LCSH: Dump trucks—Juvenile literature.
Classification: LCC TL230.15 .W34 2025 (print) | LCC TL230.15 (ebook) | DDC 629.225–dc23/eng/20240402

LC record available at https://lccn.loc.gov/2024009536
LC ebook record available at https://lccn.loc.gov/2024009537

Manufactured in the United States of America
1-1010890-53345-5/28/2024